THE

DEFENCE OF PRITHÍRAJ RASA

OF

CHANDA BARDÁÍ

No. 1.

BY

PANDIT MOHAN LÁL VISHNU LÁL PANDIA.

LIFE MEMBER OF THE ASIATIC SOCIETY OF BENGAL, ROYAL ASIATIC
SOCIETY OF GREAT BRITAIN AND IRELAND, THE GUJARAT VERNACULAR
SOCIETY, AND MEMBER AND SECRETARY TO THE STATE COUNCIL OF MEWAR,
OODEYPORE.

BENARES:

PRINTED AT THE MEDICAL HALL PRESS.

1887.

THE

DEFENCE OF PRITHÍRAJ RASÁ

OF

CHANDA BARDÁÍ

No. 1.

BY

PANDIT MOHAN LÁL VISHNU LÁL PANDIA.

LIFE MEMBER OF THE ASIATIC SOCIETY OF BENGAL, ROYAL ASIATIC
SOCIETY OF GREAT BRITAIN AND IRELAND, THE GUJARAT VERNACULAR
SOCIETY, AND MEMBER AND SECRETARY TO THE STATE COUNCIL OF MEWAR,
OODEYPORE.

BENARES:

PRINTED AT THE MEDICAL HALL PRESS.

1887.

PREFACE.

The present work has its origin in an attempt to vindicate the character and reputation of an epic much loved and respected all over the country. Love of truth and justice, predominating over all selfish ends, upholds me through all the difficulties that beset a writer of criticism. An overwhelming sense of duty incites me to enter into a field of thankless labour. But for this I would never have exposed myself to many disadvantages—taunts and ridicule—run a great risk and been lowered in the estimation of one to whom I owe a debt of gratitude. But all these sacrifices, great as they are, I can bear with patience if I have the satisfaction to know that the learned world have approved my labour and have thereby encouraged me to successfully grapple with all difficulties for the cause of truth, love and patriotism. I shall then know that I have not laboured in vain. The style of my writing has been I own a little energetic. It may seem marked by asperity but I hope that the public will .believe me when I say that nothing is so far from my heart as such an unworthy feeling—calmness and equanimity are required for the impartial investigation of truth. But if I, influenced by zeal, occasioned by the great importance of the subject treated, have in my defence brought forward any objections in a bold way—the excitement is due to the spirit of the paper which forms the basis of controversy. In the sequel of the book I have laid great stress on interpolation, and I think all the learned researchers are at one with me in this respect. In giving his opinion my learned friend F. S. Growse, Esq., C. S., M. A., says :—

"In so long a poem there are no doubt many interpolations of later date—as also there are in the Mahabharat, but it seems highly improbable that the whole work from beginning to end should be a forgery."

I have defended the points attacked by the poet laureate. Therefore no additional information can be found in the book. However it will be forthcoming in my next work when all my arguments have been well sifted and properly judged in the tribunal of learned authors.

In conclusion I have to state that this work is not an outcome of bitter personal feelings. I respect the learned poet laureate, thoroughly appreciate and value his labours when he is in his element. Moreover I am much obliged to him in personal concerns. Had it not been that the name of the prince of poets in India—one who has been commanding the heart and homage of his countrymen for centuries—is unjustly in jeopardy, I would never have taken up the pen. I am aware that my work has many defects and shall feel highly thankful if any one will show me my errors and favor me with his thoughts and suggestions.

M. V. Pandia.

THE
DEFENCE OF PRITHÍRÁJ RÁSÁ
OF
CHAND BARDÁI.

No. 1.

KAVIRÁJ SHYAMALADÁS'S PAPER, AN ATTACK ON THE ANTI-QUITY, AUTHENTICITY AND GENUINENESS OF THE EPIC CALLED THE PRITHÍRAJ RÁSÁ, COMMONLY ASCRIBED TO CHAND BARDÁI PUB-LISHED IN THE JOURNAL OF THE ASIATIC SOCIETY OF BENGAL VOL. LV. PART I. No. I—1886, WITH ITS HINDI TRANSLATION ENTITLED "PRITHIRÁJ RÁSÁ KÍ NAVÍNATÁ."

I have read this paper with great interest and careful con-sideration. Its professed object is to undeceive the public of a false impression, that the Rásá so long known to have been com-posed by Chand Bardái, is not in reality made by him, but is a deliberate forgery of the 15th or 16th century. It is not to be wondered at that a paper making so high a profession and ven-turing so much as to turn all things topsy-turvy should cause a great stir in all historical circles. A reference to most of the old books of history and to the old bards of Rájpútaná who are well versed in the Rásá has led me to think that the arguments and inferences of the Kaviraj seem to be irrelevent and un-satisfactory.

2. To those who carefully read the paper, the drift of it does but plainly indicate that the author is not to a certain extent on terms of friendship with the Bháts in general and the Cho-háns of Bedlá (1) and that he cannot bear to see the great Epic

---

(1) Our old and experienced Rájá Shiva Prasád, C. S. I., of Benares, in his letter containing his remarks on the Kaviráj's paper, says "It seems that the Kaviráj is somewhat angry with the Choháns of Bedlá."

of Chand Bardái standing in all its glory—an immortal monument of the genius of the poet—for the principle which has guided him throughout the work and which he has never lost sight of is this that the Epic may be proved false and spurious, as a mere useless production of an imaginative bard of Rájputáná. Although to help one in forming an impartial judg-ment there are passages in the Rásá which go to prove its genuineness, yet the author, I am sorry to say, has omitted them without taking them into his consideration as he should have done for the unbiased investigation of truth.

3. The author does not agree with Mr. John Beames and other learned researchers when they say that the Epic of Prithíráj Rásá was composed by Chand Bardái, the Court-bard of the last Chohán Emperor of Delhie and Ajmere, and that it is the oldest of all Hindi poems having been written in about the twelfth century. He says that the composition of the Rásá is dated later than that of the Rámáyan of Tulsidáss and Ráimall Rásá, but he is wrong as he has not shewn the exact time in which the latter two Epics were written ; he is content with simply giving his statement in a very bold and confident tone that the date of the fabrication of the former must have been between Sambat 1640 and 1670. It is worth considering that the death of Gusáin Tulsidáss took place in Sambat 1680 as is clear from the following couplet :—

दोहा ।

संवत् सोरह सै असी, असी गंग के तीर ।

सांवन सुक्का सप्तमी, तुलसी तज्यो सरीर ॥ १ ॥

Translation.

" In Sambat 1680 on the bank of the Gangá at Así on the 7th day of the waxing moon of Shrávan Tulsi left the body."

An anecdote of Tulsidáss taken from his biography (2) runs

---

(2) See Pandit Visheveswar Datta's Bhakta Mála kí Kathá and Pt. Bihárilál Chaube's Varnanábodh and Mr. E. S. Growse's valuable translation of the Ramayan.

thus :—He studied at Sorôn after he had passed his boyhood
On the death of his father he got married. Then his days passed
happily for some time. Now he performed all the duties of a
householder. A child was born to him, he was a loving husband,
greatly devoted to his wife. Once she went to her father's house
without obtaining permission of her lord. When she could not
be found at home, he went in quest of her to his father-in-law.
She read him the following verses taunting him for his love to
her :—

दोहा ।

लाज न लागत आप कों, दौरे आयेहु साथ ।
धिक् धिक् ऐसे प्रेम कों, कहा कहौं मैं नाथ ॥ १ ॥

अस्थि चर्म मय देह मम, तामों जैसी प्रीति ।
तैसी जो श्रीराम महं, होत न तौ भौ भीति ॥ २ ॥

Translation.

" Do you not feel shame, that you have come running after me
Fy ! Fy ! to your love. What shall I tell you O lord ? My body is
made of flesh and bones. The love which you have to it had you
had to Ram you would have been free from all fears or anxieties
of the world."

No sooner had he heard this than a new light broke forth,
he felt the force of her words and left the world and went to
Ayodhyá, lost in the contemplation of Rámá : here he passed
some time in meditation, having entered the holy order of Rámá-
nandees. Afterwards he settled in Káshi where he spent some
time in prayers and performances of the religious rites of his
order, on the Asi Ghát near which his *Ashrama* or abode can
still be seen. Here he used to hear the Rámáyan read out to
him and would go through it himself with love and devotion·
A little after Rámchandra appeared to him in a dream and
ordered him to compose the Rámáyan in Hindee. This led to
the composition of his famous work. Now granting that he lived
eighty years, we should consider first the marriageable age of the
Kanya Kubja Brahmans, for early marriage does not obtain among

them, and if they marry early it is not before they have attained about thirty years or so—many unmarried persons are found among them even at the age of forty—secondly the probable time of his composition of the Rámáyan after having performed all the duties of the householder. If we suppose that he composed his work while he was forty, even then the date of composition cannot be earlier than Sambat 1640. Now it is evident that even according to the opinion of the author, the above three Epics were written within the space of 40-70 years, then, how can it be proved that Rámáyan and Ráimall Rásá had been composed before ? (3). If he had searched for, and given, distinct dates of the above works, then his conjecture might have had some grounds for belief and general acceptance.

4. He says that the Epic known as the Prithíráj Rásá appears to have been fabricated by some literate Bhát of the house of Kothariyá or that of the Bedlá Choháns, both first-class nobles of Mewár, in order to show the greatness of their descent and the equality in rank of the Chohans who came from other parts of India, with the Kshatriyás of Rájpútáná. We cannot understand the cogency of the author's assertion in this respect. Histories—English, Persian and Hindi—all unite in telling us in as plain terms as ever, the high birth and power of the Choháns. Besides, the strongest of all arguments against the author

---

(3) The Kaviraj does not clearly mention in his paper what he thinks to be the date of the composition of Rámáyan. Yet it seems that Sambat 1631 is believed by him to be the correct date. He founds his belief on a verse in the Bálkanda. But how far credible are these verses is a matter of doubt for the Hindi Rámáyan shares the fate of Prithíráj Rásá and is not free from interpolations. It is there-fore that trustworthy evidence of ancient books and of the accounts of Tulsidáss from other sources than the common bázár prints is of great importance and highly essential to the finding out of truth. A great difference is observable between the Rámáyan of Tulsidáss and that of Válmíki. Many inaccuracies are found in the Prologue of the author in the Bálakánda. I do not think the date as given in the Bálakánda correct, for, discrepancies occur in the various interpolated pieces which I have been collecting for some time.

is that the Choháns of Bedlá and Kotháríyá, since they came to settle in Mewár, have been held in high esteem by the Maháránás who have given them the honor due to the highest grandees of the state, so much so that one of them offered his daughter to a Chohan noble of either of the above houses in marriage (4). This indicates their respectability. The present Maharana if asked would I hope be the most forward to testify to the truth of my assertion as regards their honor and superior rank. Therefore it was not at all necessary for them to ingratiate themselves with the princes of Mewar by the composition of the Rásá. Neither was there any necessity of the Bháts (5) singing the praises of the Maháránás, for, it does not appear that the fabrication of this Rásá has elevated them in their estimation, as history proves that they had had Jagirs before as after the composition of this great Epic.

5. The author says that the object of the writer of the Rásá in eulogising the kings of Mewár was to deceive the public into a belief in its genuineness and authenticity. Again, this is no valid proof of the Rásá being a spurious one. For the Rájás of Mewar have been almost from time immemorial famous all over India for their pure and uncontaminate blood and great power. All other Khatriyas have acknowledged their superiority and do so even at present. If the Rájás of Mewár were of common distinction the statement of the author would have been somewhat credible. But what impression can the author of a spurious book make on the public by praising one who is praised by every body?

---

(4) Intermarriage among the Hindús is a conclusive proof of the equality in rank of the house of each of the contracting parties.

(5) It is said that in Satayuga there were Velanga and Valása Bháts in the service of Chandi Devi and Shesha had Bhímsí. In Tretá, Balirám had one by name Pingal and Rámrája had Rampála. In Dwápara the Pándawas had with them Sanjaya; and in Naimisháranya, Shaunakadika had Súta. And in the present Kaliyuga Vikrama had, Vetál, Prithíraj had Chand, and Akbar, Ganga Bhát.

6. Now the author says that the fabricator has, to elude suspicion, made it known that his Epic had been composed by Chand Bardai. Again he is in error. It is hard to believe that a man who possessed learning and genius enough to compose such a masterpiece of poetry as Prithiraj Rásá should give the credit of his composition to another having no connection with it whatever. Even if we take the statement of the author to be correct, we see his own assertion disproving the truth of his proposition that there was no such poet as Chand. Moreover it proves that Chand was a distinguished poet in Prithiraj's time—one, whom to imitate, was the ambition of minor bards—; and that he has composed Prithiráj Rásá. Besides, it follows that there was a general impression at the alleged time of the fabrication that a poetical work by the name of Prithiraj Rásá existed and that it was composed by Chand. Had it not been the case, the author of the spurious poems would never have given the credit of its authorship to Chand Bardai, neither would it have been so well received all over Hindusthán.

7. The mere fact that many words of Rajputana versification and idioms peculiar to the province are found in the Rásá, does not demonstrate that the genuine author of the Epic must have been a bard of the house of Kothariyá or Bedlá Choháns, for first it is difficult to show, why the words and idioms in the Rajpútáná dialects should not have been current in the common Hindi of the time. Was there no communication between the last Hindú Emperor of Delhie and his people on the one side and the princes and men of Rajputana on the other? Was inter-marriage not prevalent between Delhie and Rajpútáná? If these things were possible then the introduction of Rajpútáná words and idioms in the vernacular of Delhie was nowise impossible. Secondly, Prithiráj and Chand were both born in Rajpútáná. Is it very strange and a thing to be wondered at if the latter should use expressions from his mother-tongue in his grand Epic? The author would have gladly withdrawn his statement had it been known to him as it is to me, that the descendants of the great bard Chand and his brother who are called Bardai, Rajorá and

Rajyorá Ráos can still be found in some of the Native States of Raj-pútáná. They still hold Jageers. Even so near as Bedlá, we see one Náthji Ráo of the above families under the protection of the Chohán noble of the place who honors him as a descendant of a house of the illustrious poet. Thirdly the use of such words as Satta, Pullyo, Chávaddisi, Utta, Páratha, Sáratha, and Bháratha सत्त फुल्यौ, चावद्दिसि, उत्त, पारत्थ, सारत्थ, भारत्थ, where letters are doubled was not a speciality in Rajpútáná, for in the heroic measure of versification it is a rule in every place in India to make redupli-cation, otherwise the metre becomes weak and languid. Besides, whenever emphasis is intended, letters are doubled even in the colloqual forms of expression. We see this in Brijá, Mainpuri, the trans-Gangetic parts, the Panjáb and other places ;—as इत्ते धर दे–उत्ते नांख दे–जबै वाकूं सत्त चढ श्रायो तबै वो सत्ती भई–हद्द मिच्च चुत्तई में डार दई–वो कै तो जाय है हट्टो बच्चो–मैंने या बात की चच्चा करी ही– सत्त हर दत्त गुरु दत्त दाता–राम राम सत्त है दो चार नित्त हैं–हम तौ भत्त्य श्रथवा भरत्थ मिलाप को मेला देखवे गये है–

The literal meaning of the word Chúka चूक is the same in all languages of India. As for its secondary signification it is various in various parts. The author's statement that its acceptation of killing or assassinating by treachery is peculiar to Rajputaná is open to contradiction. Now the word Chúk चूक has come from the Sanskrit root Chukka चुक् or Párkrit Chukkai चुक्कइ meaning to inflict pain. The original signification was "fall" "drop" (see collection of Hindi Roots by Dr. A. F. R. Hoernle J. A. S. B. vol. XLIX. Pt. I. No. II—1880 page 66). Although this use of the word is now very rare, it is no argument that it was not in vogue in other languages than that of Rajputana in the time the Rásá was composed and even much later. Here are two Gujarati ex-pressions Chúka Avavi चूक श्राववी and Chúka nákhavi चूक नाखवी in which the word Chúka is taken in this very old sense. (See Kaviraj Narmadá Shankar's Narma Kosha in Gujarati page 236 and 237). Besides this, many Sanskrit, Braj Bhásá, Prakrit, Mágha-dhi and Panjábi words and others taken from them but altered by phonetic corruption were extant in the Hindi of the time of Chand.

The author would do well to consult the comparative Grammars of the Indian languages and other philological works of Mr. John Beames, Dr. Hoernle and other authors of note. Fourthly, the language of Rajpútáná of which the author seems to be very proud, is no independent language at all, but is at least connected in every way and all respects with the dialects of Sanskrita, Hindi, Gujarati and Prakrita, &c. Then how can it claim independent phrases, words and idioms ?

8. When Mr. Beames says that the author of Prithiraj Rásá has placed Answárás over most words to make them look like Sanskrit, he does not in my humble opinion deviate from truth. But the sweeping statement of the author that because of the misplacement of Anuswárás it should be inferred that the poet had no knowledge of Sanskrit and Maghadhi—nay not even a little—is totally wrong. If we consider the corrupt state in which the work has come to our hands and compare it with its pure unpolluted condition.when fresh from the pen of the author (which we shall suppose for the sake of argument) we can in no way safely and fairly impute to him the grave charge of ignorance of the above languages. The Prithiraj Rásá of to-day is not the Prithiraj Rásá of seven centuries backwards. For even if we make allowance for poetic licence, we see the hand of time prominent in every page. So far we can safely say that the ignorance of the copyists and recensionists and the practice of writing incorrect Hindi even now obtaining in Rajputana have done much towards making the work as we have it at present. Is it therefore right to lay at the door of the poet the mistakes committed by ignorant men ? No, never. Besides it is very strange that the author should condemn Chand's poems on the ground of their having Anuswárás on the words. For the entire satisfaction of my readers I cite the following Hindi verses from the Gáyan Ságar which was published in the Sambat year 1941 = A. D. 1885 to show that up to this time the poets in India write such Hindi poems to make the language more effective. Hundreds of verses of this nature can be cited from the works of ancient and modern poets in corroboration of my statement.

When such is the case, I do not know why the author of the Prithiraj Rásá has been improperly charged with ignorance of Sanskrit by our author in the following words:—

"The author had not himself studied the language, but had apparently heard of some Maghadhi poems and to make his own composition appear ancient, he used Anuswarás; but unfortunately the words thus framed were neither Maghadhi, Hindi nor Sanskrit. It is plain from his use of Anuswarás that he was totally ignorant of Sanskrit."

(From Gáyan Ságar page 26-32.)

तनूं धुर्जटी के समानं प्रमानं । कपालं विसालं सुचंद्रं सुहानं ॥
विशालं चिनेत्रं महा काल कालं । जटा मध्य गंगा तरंगा उछालं ॥
पटं शुभ्र अंगं भुजा में भुजंगं । ग्रिवा मुंड माला सुशोभीत रंगं ॥
यही बोध रीतं बतावै सगीतं । गुनी गात गानेछ होवै पुनीतं ॥
अती है अनोपं सुगौरं स्वरूपं । पटं स्वेत धारं गले चंप हारं ॥
करे कंगनं हेम राजे बिराजे । सितं कंचुकी रंग रेशम छाजे ॥
सुठानं सिवारं सिरं बाल कालं । तनूपं छवाये सुकेशं विशालं ॥
फुलं पारिजातं सुहातं सुक्रानं । गुनी यौं बतावें बिरारी प्रमानं ॥
अती कोमलं निर्मलं हेम अंगं । पटं पीत पैने वपू शाम रंगं ॥
पटं लाल रंग महा क्रोध अंगं । सुक्रूवार वाला स्वरूपं रसालं ॥
त्रिशूलं विशालं महा काल कालं । महादेव पूजा करंति सुवालं ॥
पटं पीत भासं सदा मंद हासं । त्रिशूलं करैं शुभ रूपं उजासं ॥
पुनी चर्चितं स्रगमदं गंध भालं । अनोपं रसालं कपालं विसालं ॥
पटं शुभ्र अंगं घन श्याम रंगं । स्वरूपं सुरंगं तिया वीत संगं ॥
शुभं मस्तके कांचनीयं किरीटं । करंमें छरी पुष्प की पत्र वीटं ॥
अती चातुरं हास्य भासं विलासं । गले मुक्त माला सुजोतं उजासं ॥
करै काम केलं धरी होंस जोसं । करै गून गाने गुनी माल कौसं ॥
कपूरं सुहातं सुगंधं सुभालं । पटं शुभ्र है पद्म नेत्र विसालं ॥
रही कंचुकी स्तवरूपं रंग शामं । सदा रंग भींजी रही अंग कामं ॥

9. The author says that "Pingal is literally a treatise on Prosody" but he is wrong. Its literal meaning is a Muni—a saint by name Pingal, who was a priest of the Nagas. It was he who composed a treatise on Prosody and his work is famous. I quote as authority the following verses of Halayudha :—

श्रीमत् पिंगल नागेन्त छंद: शास्त्र महो दधेः ।
वृत्तानि मौक्तिकानिव का निचिद्दि चिनोम्यहं ॥ १ ॥
वेदानां प्रथमांगस्य कवीनां नयनस्य च ।
पिंगला चार्यसूत्रस्य मया वृत्तिर्विधास्यते ॥ २ ॥
क्षीराब्धेरमृतं यद्दद् उद्धृतं देव दानवैः ।
छन्दोऽब्धेः पिंगलाचार्य छन्दोऽमृतं तथोद्धृतं ॥ ३ ॥

If the author mentioned that the meaning given by him was metaphorical he would have been right to a certain extent. In Sanskrit the word is clear as it is called Pingala Chhanda Sutram पिंगल छंद सूत्रम्—Rules of versification by Pingal—But in Hindi the author is taken for his work. Now the thing is, the literal meaning of Pingal can never be a treatise on Prosody as the author affirms it to be. We cannot understand what he means by the expression कविता के तोल की किताब. It is very bad Hindi indeed! The Geometry of Euclid is called Euclid, but we can never say therefore that Euclid literally means a book, although the secondary signification is so, owing to the rules of rhetorical language. Again the author has made a mistake as to the meaning of Dingal. A man bearing this name flourished in the time when Magadhi and Paisháchí and other such languages began to be current in India. His rules of versification were different from those of Pingal and are known by his name.

10. The author has passed a very ruinous and annihilating sentence on Prithiraj Rásá, having founded his opinion on the inaccuracy of dates found in the work as it exists at the present time. His proof of its spuriousness chiefly rests on this. Now if his conclusion of a book being not genuine simply on the ground of mistakes in dates be accepted by the reading public to be a

universal truth, then woe to the poor authors who have racked their brains and toiled hard at their work for nothing. There may be as there are some typographical errors of dates in Tod's Rájasthán. It is therefore according to the author's hypothesis——a proof that there was no such man as Col. Tod, author of Rájasthán, that Tod's Rájasthán is a mere forgery and that it has been composed by an English knowing minstrel in the pay of the Maharana, as it contains many eulogies of the Rajás of Mewar. The author should have taken it for granted that Chand wrote true dates both in words and figures, but that clerical mistakes have crept in during so long a time as seven centuries, much to the detriment of the work. When such is the case the readings of the same passages become different in different MSS. vide the author's quotation :—

शाक सु विक्रम सत्त शिव अठ अग्ग पंचास

On the word atha अठ the Editor A. S. J. writes a note to the following effect :—

"In the author's version we see atha अठ; in another Pancha पंच; while Tod gives a different reading."

Was Chand or the writer of the spurious Rásá accountable for the above different readings ?

11. The author, in ascertaining the truth about the Sambat 1158 of the last battle of Prithiraj which we find in the Rásá of the day, has taken, according to his own choice, the two Persian histories, viz. "Abul Fida" and "Tubakat-i-Nasari" as his most reliable authorities to caution the public against the inaccuracies of dates in the Epic but the former does not sufficiently answer the purpose of our author because he himself says that "It does not mention any thing about Prithiraj's battle." Accordingly I put aside "Abul Fida" our author's nominal authority untouched. And I take under consideration the latter "Tabakat-i-Nasari." The Minhaj-i-Saraj in the reign of Shahab-ud-din at one place has given H. 588=A. D. 1192 for this battle but at the other he mentions that in this year Shahab-ud-din fought with Sultan Sháh! Likewise in H. 581=A. D. 1185 he says that Shahab-ud-din

again led an army against Lahore and in the reign of Khusro
Mallik he himself says that Muiz-ud-din made only two expedi-
tions on Lahore i. e. one in H. 577 and the other when it was
finally taken in H. 583! If the author would take the trouble of
perusing the English translation of the "Tabakat-i-Nasari" by
Major Raverty with his valuable foot-notes, I am sure, he would
come to know that this authority also is not such an infallible one as
he has considered it to be. Because the Minhaj-i-Saraj often makes
such mistakes which for a writer of so early a period is certainly
a matter of great regret; it seems that he had such a bad memory
that he has said something at one place and at the other he himself has contradicted the same. He has made mention of his
father's appointment as Kazi at one place but in the list of Kazies
we do not find his name. How unfairly Shahab-ud-din obtained
Uchchah, he has altogether left unnoticed and there are many discrepancies where he has enumerated the victories, successes and
holy-wars of Muiz-ud-din. He is a great exaggerator also. He
says that in the treasury of Ghazni there were actually fifteen
hundred *mans* of diamonds alone and at the same time he directs
us to judge of other jewels and money accordingly. If we take
his *man* to be a Tabriz *man* which is equal to about 2 lbs. or one
seer, still his statement seems highly improbable. I do not know
why the author has approved the Minhaj-i-Saraj alone rejecting
the other contemporary writers as Hasan Nizami and others. Is
it not the reason that they differ in the facts at issue? As the
author has himself admitted that the writer of the "Tabakat-i-
Nasari" has made a good many mistakes in the names, consequent-
ly I do not take them under my criticism. I hope that my
readers are well aware that all accounts of Shahab-ud-din's reign
written by Minhaj-i-Saraj are as hearsay evidence in proof of the
matter under dispute. Because he was born in H. 589 and he has
himself mentioned in his book that in H. 624 he first set foot
in Hind. I do not accept as true the Sambat 1248-49 of Prithiraj's last battle on the Tabakat's authority alone, as the author has
done, but on that of the majority of Persian histories and of
the modern researches. Now it remains to say that it would not

be improper if the author would accept either that the real Chand has written true dates in the Rásá but they have been made incorrect in so long a time by the fault of revisers or recensionists (as a majority of learned scholars think them to be as numerical errors) or what I have advocated in my conclusion.

12. Our author attacks Col. Tod in the following words :—

"Colonel Tod has given Sambat 1249 for the battle between Shahab-ud-din and Prithiraj; but he does not adduce any arguments against Sambat 1158 given in the Prithiraj Rásá."

Had he formed his opinion as he should have done, after having carefully gone through the volumes of the Colonel, whose work was a labour of love and who maturely weighed all matters given therein he would not have hazarded such a statement. I refer him to Col. Tod's Rajasthán vol. II. page 420 foot-note 2 which reads as follows :—

"The Hárá chronicle says S. 981, but by some strange, yet uniform error all the tribes of Chohans antedate their chronicles by a hundred years. Thus Beesaldeo's taking possession of Auhulpur Pattan is "nine hundred fifty, thirty and six" (S. 986) instead of S. 1086. But it even pervades Chand, the poet of Prithiraj, whose birth is made 1115 instead of S. 1215; and here in all probability, the error commenced by the ignorance (wilful we cannot imagine) of some rhymer."

Cannot our author guess Colonel Tod's opinion of the authenticity of the dates of the Prithiraj Rásá from the above foot-note ?

13. Colonel Tod has written that Ráná Rahap, grandson of Ráwal Samar Singh, reigned in the 13th century of Vikrami era. But the author places his reign in the 4th part of the 14th century. But I cannot persuade myself into believing his statement until I see it corroborated by the evidence of such learned researchers as Mr. John Beames, Dr. Hoernle and Dr. R. Mittra. The ground our author treads is very delicate and slippery for it relates to the genealogy of the Maharanas of Mewar. He has drawn up a table of genealogy according to his mind. I fear it is not so

very correct as he pretends it to be. Unless, therefore, I find it approved after a critical examination and accepted as true by the gentlemen mentioned above, I can never have sufficient reason to be satisfied with it, the more so as it does not tally with the table of Col. Tod and the dates given by Dr. Hunter and Mr. Forbes. Even granting that the latter are wrong in this respect, it does not follow that the whole Rásá is a forgery.

14. It seems strange how Prithiraj Rásá alone could have misled all historians, Bháts, and Barwás, for what has been written in English histories was not taken solely from the Prithiraj Rásá but from other sources too, after a careful consideration of all facts and never in an off-hand manner. It is not that the home-records of the Rajputana chiefs and princes have been written only on the authority of the Rásá. Ask a Barwá, Bhát or Cháran and he will give you a plain artless answer to the following effect:— "Bápaji, Here are the Sambats, dates and genealogical tables as they have been written by our fathers; once Colonel Tod saw them and told us that there were inaccuracies in such and such places. If there be any mistakes, correct them. Whatever may be the errors in our Rásás we do not say that the responsibility rests with the author but with the copyists and some evil intending or malicious men, who might well be suspected of altering the dates to answer their purpose."

15. The conclusion drawn by the author from the inscription stone at Bijoli, dated S. 1226, in which no mention is made of the Chohan kings of Ajmere after Someswara, that Prithiraj did not ascend the throne till that year, seems incorrect. The reason is that Prithiraj having gone to Delhie and been adopted in the line of Taur kings, his name could not with propriety have been written among the Chohan kings of Ajmere. The author's conjecture that Prithiraj may have been crowned king of Delhie within 42 days after the date of the inscription is founded on the testimony of another stone at Mainálgarh erected on the 15th of the dark half of Chaitra in Sambat 1226. Here the author is in my humble opinion totally in the wrong. Because the inscription stone found by Colonel Skinner at Hansi in 1818 A. D., bearing

date the Sambat 1224 and presented by him to Lord Hastings, the Governor General of India, was of the time in which Prithiraj reigned in Delhie. Portions of this inscription have been published in the Transactions vol. I of the Royal Asiatic Society of Great Britain and Ireland. Besides the above, another stone got in a place in the Palace of Firoze Shah in Delhie had the year Sambat 1220 engraved on it. Having a great antiquarian interest it was minutely and critically examined by learned researchers and became of great service to them in fixing the year of Prithiraj's accession to the throne in Sambat 1220. In addition to the evidence of the inscriptions, the following extract from Col. Tod's Rajasthán vol. I page 80 bears out my statement:—

" Delhie, the ancient Indraprastha, founded by Udhishthar and which tradition says lay desolate for eight centuries, was rebuilt and peopled by Anungpal Tuar in Sambat 848 (A. D. 792) who was followed by a Dynasty of twenty princes, which concluded with the name of the founder Anungpál in Sambat 1220 (A. D. 1164) when contrary to the Salic law of the Rajpoots, he abdicated (having no issue) in favor of his grandchild the Chohan Prithiraj."

16. It is strange that the author does not think that Samarsi was married with Prithá Bái' sister to the Emperor Prithiraj. Here he obstinately holds to his disbelief in spite of all incontrovertible proof to the contrary. The reason of his dogmatism appears to be his desire to see the Rásá fall to the ground and be proved spurious for if he would admit their marriage to be a true fact he would be placed in a false position because Samarsi would then be proved to be a contemporary of Prithiráj. Now an inscription stone set up by the orders of Maháráná Ráj Singh on the Rájsamudra gives the following testimony as to the marriage of Pritha Bai with Samar Singh.

ततः समरसिंहाख्यः पृथ्वीराजस्य भूपतेः ।
पृथाख्याया भगिन्यास्तु पतिरित्यति हार्दतः ॥

Translation.

"Samar Singh was husband of Pritha, sister to the Emperor Prithiraj."

As the author has not found fault with the above inscription, I am led to believe that he accepts it to be trustworthy. But I am afraid he might try to shew it to be false like Prithiraj Rásá on the ground of its not bearing out his own hypothesis. Secondly another circumstance which can never be disproved or set aside as false is the settlement of the Sanáwar or Sanádhya Brahmans &c. in Mewar. That they came for the first time to live in this part of Rajpútáná, in the train of Pritha Bái, the lands held by their descendants to this day sufficiently testify.

17. The cause which has led the author to point out and prove the spuriousness of the Prithiráj Rásá and the inaccuracies contained in the history of Mewar and other parts of India, lies in his assumption that Samar Singh neither lived in the age of Prithiráj nor did he marry the sister of the latter. On the evidence of several inscriptions it is proved by him that from Sambat 1332 to 1344 was the time in which Samar Singh may have flourished. I shall now criticise the testimony of the inscriptions and prove with the concurrence of many influential Chiefs, Pandits, Bháts and Charans, the author's caste fellows, that Samar Singh was a contemporary of his brother-in-law the Emperor Prithiraj Chohan of Delhie.

18. The mere mention of the name Maháráj Tej Singh on an inscription stone found on the bridge of Gambhiri a stream flowing down the fort of Chitor, bearing date the Sambat 1324 has bewildered the author and led him astray into hastily identifying the hero of the inscription with Ráwal Tej Singh father of Samar Singh. Had the author arrived at an unbiased decision having calmly and carefully considered all matters in connection with the name he would not have been deceived by such a chance coincidence. Now let us see for a moment the title prefixed to the name. The mere title of Maharaj has never been found inserted before the name of any of the Maharanas of

Mewar on any inscription stone. Even if we suppose for the sake of argument that in some instances such has been the case, then we must invariably see the name defined at length with terms peculiar to the house, so there remains no difficulty in making out who the Maharana was. Besides, the inscription under discussion is a strange one. It does not go the common way of all such records. Its drift cannot he clearly made out. So long as other inscriptions are not forthcoming to corroborate this one I do not find sufficient reason to disbelieve the generally accepted age of Samarsi.

19. I shall now examine the other three inscriptions quoted by the author. The first found on the bridge of the Gambhiri bearing date the 13th of the bright half of the month of Jetha in Sambat 13—2; the 2nd contained the date of Thursday the 5th of the waxing moon in Vaishakh in 1335 and the 3rd the bright half of Vaishakh in 1344 recording the grant of land in honor to the temple of the god Vaijnath. It appears that they have the same character with the Prithiraj Rásá in disgrace. The dates in the latter are a century earlier than the real ones while those of the former are later by a hundred years. On enquiring of the respectable and well informed people here, into the causes of this difference, I have come to learn that some calumniator has been guilty of interpolation, by the insertion of 3 in place of two. I have no reason to disbelieve the opinion, for by changing 3 into 2 we arrive at the true age of Samar Singh. Secondly because in the face of their convincing statement that of our author and researcher truly falls to the ground. To be sure the various dates were 1232, 1235, and 1244; as the inscription stone at the temple of Samarsi at Mainal dated S. 12—2. testifies. Further these inscriptions appear to be Surahs and as such cannot be relied on in as much as many counterfeit Surahs have been set up and Copper-plates engraved by avaricious men for holding lands in charity. Admitting that the inscription stones alluded to by the Kaviraj are not false, we may think that they having been raised many years after the events recorded thereon had taken place might contain incorrect dates.

20. Now the inscription on a stone near the temple of Achaleswar Mahadeva on Mount Abú remains to be seen. As to its date which is the 1st day of the waxing moon in Mragsir in Sambat 1342 all the respectable Pandits and Bhats here are at one in their opinion that it was the year not of Maharana Samar Singh's repairing the temple but of the erection of the stone. Not being satisfied with what they said I consulted some of my friends, learned Pandits of Benares—on the matter. The result of my investigation has confirmed the truth of the statement made by the natives. An impartial view of my argument and conjectures such as have hitherto been made and will in future be given in these pages will enable a man to see that my native friends are right. Read the inscription from 46th sloka to its end. You will then know that the date shews the time of the inscription stone being erected. The expression प्रशस्ति: कृता: bears out my assertion. It does not unfrequently happen that a building is erected at a time and the inscription relating to it is set up years after. Besides it is no wonder that it may have suffered from interpolation and thus shared the fate of the above three of its kind. Moreover I admit that the remarks of Dr. Hoernle on the inaccuracy of the Sambat of this inscription as well as on the allusion contained in the 46th verse of it are not wrong but highly probable. He says :—

"He (Rawal Samar Si) is mentioned in an old Sanskrit inscription which professes to have been written during his reign, in commemoration of a temple erected by Samar Si on the sacred Mount Abú. A notice and translation of the inscription by H. H. Wilson is given in the Asiatic Researches vol. XVI. pp. 284, 291—298. No. X. He is there (verse 46) said to have delivered the kingdom of Gurjara from the Turushka (Mohomedan) armies. This probably refers to Sahabuddin's unsuccessful invasion of Gujarat in A. D. 1178, when he was defeated by Bhimdeva who at that time was crown-prince under his brother Múlráj, King of Gujarat (see Forbes Rás Málá vol. I page 207) and seems to have had Samar Singh as his ally. There is however, an error in the date of the inscription; it is given as Sambat

1342, which would be A. D. 1285; a date much too late for Samar Singh. There seems to be an error of exactly 100 years; for the date A. D. 1185 would suit very well. Probably the date on the inscription should be Sambat 1242=A. D. 1185." (vide Dr. Hoernle's Prithiráj Rásau in English Pt. II Fas. I page 31, foot-note 187).

21. Thus there are conflicting opinious of the inscriptions given by the author. Now in support of the truth of my assertion I shall cite the following incontrovertible and unconflicting proofs.

A. At Mainal there is a temple of Samarsi. The inscription-stone attached to this place bears the date of S. 12—2. It contains the praises of Samarsi and Arnoraj and mention is made of Prithiraj. A reference to the page 686 of the Vol. II of Colonel Tod's Rájasthán will cost the reader no pains worth the name :—

"In the Mandir of Samarsi, we found the fragment of another inscription dated S. 12—2. And containing the eulogy of Samarsi and Arnoraj, lord of the region, also the name of Prithiráj who "destroyed the barbarians" and concluding with Sanwat Singh."

B. The large inscription-stone on the lake of Rájsamudra dated 15th Magh Sudi Sambat 1722 set up by the orders of the Government of Mewar, contains the following verses, the truth of which has not been questioned either by the author or any other man :—

ततः समरसिंहाख्यः पृथ्वीराजस्य भूपतेः ॥

पृथाख्याया भगिन्यास्तु पतिरित्यति हार्देतः ॥ २४ ॥

गोरी साहिब दीनेन गज्जनीशेन संगरं ।

कुर्वंतो ऽखर्वं गर्वस्य महासामंत शोभिनः ॥ २५ ॥

दिल्लीश्वरस्य चोहान नाथस्यास्य सहायकृत् ।

सद्वादश सहस्रैः स्ववीराणां सहितो रणे ॥ २६ ॥

Translation.

"Then Samar Singh, being the husband of king Prithiráj's sister, named Pritha, rendered aid, through great affection, with his 12000 heros, to Chohan—nátha (i. e. Prithiraj) the lord of Delhi, who, being very proud and distinguished by his powerful feudatory princes, was waging war with Gori-Sahiba-dina, the king of Gajjani."

C. In a Manuscript entitled the Bhikhá Rásá it is written that Samar Singh flourished in the time of Prithiraj. That he married the sister of the last Chohan Emperor and helped his brother-in-law in his war with Shab-ud-din Gory. I have been long on the look out for this history, but regret to say no success has attended my efforts. Strange to mention that the Bhats and Charuns of Rajputaná go the length of denying its existence. I remember to have sent a copy of this Manuscript to Sir John Muir at the request of his nephew, Col. J. W. J. Muir, Political Agent of Harouti and Tonk, having bought it of a Bhát at Jhalawar for Rs. 15. I read what I have written above of Samarsi in the M. S. While regretting very much my inability to procure this book I fortunately came across the following couplet in which reference is made to the Manuscript :—

बध्वा गोरि पतिं दैवात् । स्वयांतः सूर्ये बिंब भित् ॥
भीखा रासा पुस्तकेस्य । यदुस्योक्तोस्ति विस्तरः ॥ २७ ॥

Translation.

"Took Gori-pati captive in battle, and, through Fate, went to heaven (i. e. died) penetrating the solar disk. A description at length of this battle is given in the work, Bhikha Rásá."

D. Every one in Mewar both high and low, rich and poor knows that Bâí Prithá was married to Maháráná Samar Singh and that the following castes came over in the train of the bride.

(1) Sanáwar or Sanádhya Bráhmans.

(2) Daipurá Mahájans.

(3) Rajora Raos &c.,

To this day their descendents hold Jagirs or rent free lands, simply for the reason of their fore-fathers' settlement in Mewar. They take it ill if any one question the truth of their coming over in Pritha's following—a fact which they look upon as a point of honor—Therefore I value this as a universally accepted proof of Samar Singh's being in the period of Prithiráj.

E. Likewise do I value Col. Tod's writings as an authority in historical and antiquarian matters. He dates the birth of Samarsi in Sambat 1206 and his statement agrees with the inscription at the temple of Samarsi at Mainal. He writes the account of Samar Singh's life, at length. If he had the least doubt in his mind and met with any conflicting opinion he would never have been satisfied until he had turned over all stones, sifted all matters and arrived at the truth. Alas! there is no Colonel Tod now to write the history of Rajputana!!!

F. The second proof in support of my assertion is the writing of Colonel Tod in his personal narrative page 682 vol. 2 in his paragraph containing a brief account of the buildings of Mainal on the 21st February when he was on the spot in the course of his annual tour. In his brief description of the buildings of Prithiraj and Samarsi the following account appears. Is it not a convincing proof of Samar Singh's flourishing in the time of Prithiraj?

" On the very brink of the precipice overhanging the abyss is the group of mixed temples and dwellings which bear the name of Prithiraj; while those on the opposite side are distinguished by that of Samarsi of Chitor, the brother-in-law of the Chohan Emperor of Delhie and Ajmere whose wife Pritha Bai, has been immortalized by Chand, with her husband and brother. Here, the grand cleft between them, these two last bulwarks of the Rajpoot races were accustomed to meet with their families and pass days of affectionate intercourse, in which no doubt the political condition of India was a prominent topic of discussion. If we may believe, and we have no reason to distrust, the testimony of Chand, had Prithiraj listened to the Counsels of the Ulysses

4

of Hindús (in which light Samarsi was regarded by friend and foe) the Islamite never would have been lord of Hindusthán."

22. Kaviraj makes much of the difference between the dates of the Jeypore, Jodhpore and Boodi Kings. But this uniform difference of one hundred years or so in the genealogical writings of Barwa, Bhat, and Charuns, can be easily accounted for if the antiquarians and researchers assume as true what I have stated elsewhere in detail and what is generally the opinion of genealogists.

23. The author says that there could be no copying or rhyming errors on four different grounds. Although the reasonings are not valid and can be easily contradicted, yet for satisfaction I shall review them in order.

A. If we read the following verses having corrected the copying and rhyming errors therein supposed to contain for the sake of argument we see that the metre does not become defective and weak as the author has presumed.

For	Read
एकादश से पंच दह	द्वादश से पंच दह
संवत् इक्क दस पंच अग	संवत् दुक्क दस पंच अग
एकादश संबतह	द्वा दस संबतह
ग्यारह से अठतीस भनि	बारह से अरू बीस भनि
ग्यारह से अठतीसा मानं	बारह से अरू बीसा मानं
ग्यारह से चालीस	बारह से चालीस
ग्यारह से इक्यावने	बारह से चालीस इक्क
एकादश से सत्त ⎱	द्वा दस से सत्त ⎱
अठुपंचास अधिकतर ⎰	अठु चालीस अधिकतर ⎰

B. If we take Shiva and Hara to be the errors either of copyists or of any interpolator but not of the celebrated Chand himself and substitute Ravi in their place the quantity of the verse remains all the same. Ravi means twelve.

For	Read
संवत् हर चालीस	संवत् रवि चालीस
शाक सुविक्रम सत्तशिव	शाक सुविक्रम सत्त रवि

C. The author is right when he says that in the MSS. of the Rásá written a hundred years or two ago as well as in those of the day, the reading is S. 1100. But the uniformity and consistency of this date does not go to prove the author's conclusion of the spuriousness of the Rásá. Because as the reading of 1100 occurs uniformly, so according to the researches of the English antiquarians, the difference of one hundred is uniform. When we have seen that two inscriptions of the time of Prithiraj, bearing date the Sambats 1220 and 1224 respectively have been found by the researchers. what harm could there possibly be in ascribing the errors of mistakes in dates to a recensionist, a poet or a copyist.

D. If the true astronomical date reckoned from the position of the stars at the time of Prithiraj's birth-date found in his horoscope, does not correspond with that given in the Rásá it does not follow that the Epic is not genuine. For when it is assumed that the date of the birth of Prithiraj was wrong, by analogy we can rightly and safely think that there may be mistakes as to the day, month, star, hour and minutes of his birth, for if the data be wrong the quesita must be naturally so. The Pandit Narayandeva Shastry is not to blame, for when the question put to him was wrong how could the answer be right. It would have been well if the Kaviraj had asked the Pandits to rectify the errors in the horoscope.

24. It is greatly to be regretted that the author insists that Chand was not the court-bard of either Rájá Someswardeva or Prithiraj, and writes in his original Hindi book that the existence of the bard Chand Bardai is known only from Prithiraj Rásá—I am therfore obliged to quote the following conclnding verses from a poetical work named Drishta-kuta-ki-Tiká of the famous Hindi poet Súrdáss in contradiction to the authors sweeping statement. Do they not prove that Chand was the court-bard of Prithiraj ?

पद *

प्रथम ही प्रथ जगत में प्रगट अद्भुत रूप ।
ब्रह्मराव बिचारि ब्रह्मा राख नाम अनूप ॥

पानपथ देवी दियो सिव आदि सुर सुख पाय ।
कह्यो दुर्गा पुत्र तेरो भयो अति अधिकाय ॥

पारि पायन सुरन के सुर सहित अस्तुति कीन ।
तासु बंस प्रसिद्ध में भौ चन्द चारु नवीन ॥

भूप पृथ्वीराज दीन्हो तिन्हैं ज्वाला देस ।
तनय ताके चार कीन्हो प्रथम आप नरेस ॥

दूसरे गुनचन्द तासुत सीलचंद सरूप ।
बीरचन्द प्रताप पूरन भयो अद्भुत रूप ॥

रन्तभार हमीर भूपत सङ्ग खेलत आय ।
तासु बंस अनूपभौ हरिचन्द अति बिख्याय ॥

आगरे रही गोपचल में रही तासुत बीर ।
पुत्र जनमे सात ताके महा भट्ट गम्मीर ॥

कृष्णचन्द उदारचन्द नु रूपचन्द सुभाइ ।
बुद्धिचन्द प्रकाश चोषो चंद भे सुख दाइ ॥

देवचन्द प्रबोध संस्तुत चंद ताको नाम ।
भयो सप्तो नाम सूरजचन्द मन्द निकाम ॥

सो समर करि स्याहि सेवक गए बिधके लोक ।
रच्छो सूरजचन्द द्रगतें हीन भर बर सोक ॥

परो कूप पुकार काहू सुनीना संसार ।
सातयें दिन आइ जदुपति कीन आपु उधार ॥

दियो चखदै कही सिसु सुनु मांग बर जो चाइ ।
हों कही प्रभु भगति चाहत सज्जनाम सु भाइ ॥

दूसरो ना रूप देखो देखि राधा स्याम ।

सुनत करुना सिन्धु भाखी एव मस्तु सु धाम ॥

प्रबल दच्छिन बिप्र कुलते सचु है हे नास ।

अषित बुधि विचारि विद्या मान मानें सास ॥

नाम राखे मोर सूरजदास सूर सुश्याम ।

भए अन्तर धान बीते पाछली निसि जाम ॥

मोहि पनसां इहै ब्रज की बसे सुख चित थाप ।

थापि गोसांई करी मेरी आठ (2) मद्दु छाप (2) ॥

बिप्र प्रथ जगात को है भाव भूरि निकाम ।

सूर है नंदनन्द जूको लयो मोल गुलाम ॥

Translation.

First in the Jagát family was born an admirable image.

Whom Brahmá having duly considered, well named as Brahma Rao.

Devi gave him suck and Shiva &c. all the gods felt pleased.

Durgá said your son is born to be a great (man),

And praised him with the Sura of Surás in unlimited terms.

In his famous family the beautiful and fortunate Chand was born.

To whom the emperor Prithiraj gave Jwálá Desh.

The first of all his (Chand's) four sons he (Prithiraj) made Naresha (Poet Laureate).

His (Chand's) second son's son was Silachand.

Bírchand had been an incomparable being possessing energy.

He played with Hamir the king of Rantabhár.

In his family the very famous well-named Harichand was born.

---

(2) Ashtá Chhápa i. e. the eight chosen great Poet-musicions namely Súrdás, Kumbhanadás, Parmananddás, Krishnadás, Chhita Swami, Govind Swami, Chaturbujadás, and Nandadás.

He (having) lived at Agra, his son Birchand lived at Gopachal.

Seven sound and brave sons were born to him.

Krishnachand, Udarchand, and Rupachand, good brothers.

Budhichand born the fourth son giving happiness.

Devachand and the intelligent whose name is Sansratchand.

The seventh I Surajchand a stupid and useless (child).

The others ('dying) in the Military service of the Emperors, went to the region of god.

I, the blind Surajchand remained greatly afflicted.

I fell into a well and no one in the world heard my prayers.

On the seventh day the Yadupati having appeared there took m out of it.

Having given me eye sight, He said, O boy! hear me ask what boon you want.

I replied, O Lord! I want thy devotion and the name of enemies is unbearable to me.

Having seen the image of Shyáma, the lord of Rádhá, I don't want to see any other image.

Hearing this the Ocean of mercy (Krishna) having determined said, So be it.

The enemies shall he destroyed by a powerful Brahman family of Deccan.

The wise, having considered this by supernatural understanding accept this as true.

The good Shyám (Krishna) named me (Surajdas) Sur.

And disappeard at the decline of night.

There is an open saying of my living in Braj from childhood.

The Gosain placed me among the (ashthachápa) eight chosen Great Poets.

My much useless name is of the famous Sacerdotal Jagat caste

Súr is a purchased slave of Nadanandaji (son of Nand, Krishna).

Moreover the Persian and Jamūn histories give evidence to the effect that Chand lived in the time of our last Hindú Emperor, and that he was his devoted admirer and friend. If I take extracts from the original books and cite them here I fear that our book would be too lengthy. Therefore I quote the following lines from Major Raverty's note to give a general idea of the fact in a few lines only. The following lines not only corroborate the fact of Chand's being in the alleged time but they also confirm a few other facts with a slight difference, mentioned in his great Epic under defence :—

(Major Raverty's Tabakat-i-Nasiri page 486.)

"The Hindús give a different account, which is also related by Abul-Fazl, and in the Jamūn History with a slight difference :— "Although the Persian Chroniclers state that Ráe Pithora fell on the field of Taláwari (Tarain), and that Muizz-ud-din fell at Damyak by the hand of a Khokhar who had devoted himself to the deed, and that such statement has been followed by the author of the Tabakat-i-Akbari and by Firishtah, nevertheless, from the mouth of the Hindi bards, the depositaries of the traditions of every celebrated event, and which is handed down orally from generation to generation, it is stated that, after Rae Pithora was made captive and taken to Ghaznin, one Chanda, some write Chāndā, the confidential follower and eulogist of Rae Pithora, styled by some authors his Court poet, proceeded to Ghaznin to endeavour to gain information respecting his unfortunate master. By his good contrivances he managed to get entertained in Sultán Muizz-ud-din's service, and succeeded in holding communication with Rae Pithora in his prison. They agreed together on a mode of procedure, and one day Chandā succeeded by his cunning in awakening the Sultán's curiosity about Rae Pithora's skill in archery, which Chandā extolled to such a degree that the Sultán could not restrain his desire to witness it, and the captive Rajah was brought out and requested to show his skill. A bow and arrows were put into his hands, and, as agreed upon, instead of discharging his arrow at the mark, he transfixed the Sultán, and he died on the spot, and Rae Pithora and Chandá were cut to pieces then and there by the Sultán's attendants.

The Jamún History states that Rae Pithora had been blinded (see note 1 page 466) and that, when brought forth, and his own bow and arrows given him, notwithstanding his blindness, having fitted an arrow, and tried the temper of the bow, guided by the sound of the Sultan's voice, and the indications of Chandā, he discharged the arrow in the right direction, and transfixed him. The rest agrees."

25. The author has written that in the time that Udaya Singh of Marwar was in attendance at the Court of Akbar, the bards of Marwar often kept communication with Delhie and began to visit the Imperial city and some distinguished Hindi poets flourished such as Tulsidáss, Keshodáss Súrdáss, Iswardáss, Barats Lakha and Narhardass and others. I cannot agree with the author in reducing all the above named poets to a common level for there is vast difference between the genius of Súrdáss, Tulsidass and that of Barats Lakha and Narhardáss. I hope the following couplet is known to the author :—

दोहा

सूर सूर्ज तुलसी ससी । उड़गन केसो दास ॥
और कवी खज्जोत सम । जहँ तहँ करत प्रकाश ॥

Translation.

"Súrdáss is as the Sun; Tulsidas the moon; Keshodas a star but other poets are like glow-worms—they show their tiny light here and there."

Besides these poets did not flourish in one age as the author says they did. I shall ascertain the time of Súrdás only by way of example. It is clear from the sacred books of the Vallabhácharyan sect that the Pontiff Founder Vallabhacharya came for the first time at Brija in Sambat 1548-49 for proclaiming the manifestation of Shreenathji on the Giriraj mountain. On his way to Muttra he halted on the Gaughat between Agra and Muttra. There was the seat of the Swami Súrdás. He had made many followers and his name, as a great poet, had spread far and wide all over India. Both the priests here met and Súrdáss with all his disciples became the follower of Vallabha-charya. Now the former was taken to Giriraj. The latter having proclaimed the appearance of Shrinathji appointed him the head of Ashthachápa or the chosen eight. Vallabhacharya got libera-tion from flesh in 1587 and in a short time the Head Poet-Musician followed him and joined in the eternal ring with Krishna Now this fact is worthy of note that Surdás was a poet-musi-cian and not like others a mere poet. He had the unique genius of a singer. His meeting with Vallabhacharya must have been while he was at least fifty. Adding fifty years more to his life we see that the author's date of 1639 is wrong. In this manner as it is evident that Súrdás flourished before Sambat 1600, the author's affirmation regarding the introduction of Persian words in the writings of the Hindi poets is incorrect. Examine the following verses of Surdás and you will at once know how Persian words were extant in the composition of Hindi poets even before the year 1639 as mentioned by the author :—

राग भैरव

चलना रे प्रभु के दरबार । कालबली ठाड़ो चोबदार ॥

इन हजूर में याद तिहार । चलने की कछु करो तयार ॥

जिस में हुरमत रहै तुमार । ऐसी करनी करले यार ॥

जिस को खाविंद पकड़ बुलावै । जतन करे कछु बन नहीं आवै ॥

बिन मरजी कोई रहन न पावै । क्या गरीब क्या साह कहावै ॥

जब जम आवै कछुन बसावै । छिन में बांध पकर लेजावै ॥

तब तो तू कछु कौन छुड़ावै । ठिंग बैठा कलपै कल पावै ॥

मौजूदात की तयारी कीजै । दरसन तलब बेग चल लीजै ॥

जो खाविंद तोहि देख पसीजै । कंठ लगाय रंग में भीजै ॥

करनी का कर कमर कटारा । सील सिपर तप तेग तुमारा ॥

धरै तोष कर ध्यान पियारा । ज्ञान घोड़ हूजै असवारा ॥

जो तू ऐसा होय चलैगा । मालिक मन में बहुत खिलैगा ॥

काम क्रोध मद लोभ मोहमद । यह संसार सपन दहैगा ॥

निसवासर हरि नांम उचार कै । रसना जपले परम पद लहैगा ॥

सूरदास सुख जो तू चाहै । गोबिन्द के गुण ज्या तू गावै ॥

पतित उधार बिरद कहावै । चरण शरण नति ध्यावै ॥ १ ॥

26. Among the most potent arguments of the author in proof of the spuriousness of the Prithiraj Rásá it is found that the proportion of Persian words to Hindi in the Epic is 1 : 10 To test the accuracy of his statement, I have counted all the words in the Canto of Devagiri in Dr. Hoernle's Edition of the Rásá. Out of about 2973 words thirty are found to be Persian :—" Mír Banda, Surtan, Sillah, Gajjanesh, Gori, Sahib, Khán, Hossein, Durbar and Furmán, &c." Now the ratio of 30 to 2973 is as 1 : 99·1—very insignificant indeed. From this calculation my readers can infer the value of our author's arguments. Besides, I ask him what Hindi words could Chand have written in place of those quoted above ?

27. The author has founded his assertion of the Rásá being composed sometime between Sambat 1640 and 1670 on the signification of a few verses as :—

कलंकियां राय केदार ।

पापियां राय प्रयाग ।

हत्यारां राय बाणारसी ।

मद्यपान राय राजानरी गंगा ।

सुलतान यहण मोलन ।

सुलतान मान मलन ।

His statement that the verses allude to Rana Sangrám Singh and not to Ráwal Samar Singh contemporary with Prithiraj—is far fetched, conjectural and quite opposed to the meaning of the poet—

for why should he while eulogizing the latter dwell on the merits of
the former, one who was born centuries afterwards. I wonder
what has our learned critic seen in these lines justifying his hasty
conclusion, and proving that the Rásá was a production of the
16th century. In the face of all evidence to the contrary—in the
face of the plain meaning of the lines, a meaning which lies on
the surface—in the face of all consistency as to time and place—
he thus boldly misinterprets the allusion by a great strain of im-
agination to shew the spuriousness of the immortal Epic. The
bards of Rajpootana who are not like-minded with our critic, see
no reason why these lines should refer to Rana Sagram Singh and
not to Rawal Samar Singh as is obvious. Even if we admit that
his meaning is correct, we are struck with the fallacy of his argument because the verses might come from the pen of a modern
poet and yet prove the genuineness of the Prithiraj Rásá.

Now as regards the following couplet containing the prophecy, there is a show of plausibility in the argument of the

सोरह से सत्तातरे विक्रम साऋ बदीत ।
दिल्ली धर चित्ताड पत ले खग्गां बल जीत ॥

author. First the grammatical construction is plain to a common observer indicating that this is a prophecy. It may be
that a poet, fired with zeal and earnestness, sometimes com-
poses a rhapsody. Here in the case before us we may reject
the prophecy as false for the mere style of the verses goes
to prove that they are not genuine as they have not the grace
and elegance of the writing of Chand. Secondly the logical inference of the Kaviraj takes us by surprise, he says that " here
the poet delivers a prophecy that the King of Chitore would take
Delhie. Therefore it is quite evident that the couplet and hence
the poem was written some time before Sambat 1677." It passes
our understanding and all the rules of just reasoning how if a
part of a thing is wrong, the whole is wrong. The confident way
in which the conclusion has been given seems to show that the
author thinks that a part is equal to the whole, a reasoning un-
precedented and unparalleled in the history of thought. Now

according to the axiom laid down by the author, we should learn to think that because the Crown rupee is some carats copper the whole coin is made of that metal—because a sentence or two of the learned Dr. Mittra's Antiquities of Orissa are of questional truth the whole volume—nay both of them are quite incorrect. When our author from this prophetic couplet which contains the word Chitor make his own inference according to his pleasure, why can not a Mewati draw a different one on the ground that Tod's MS. has "Mewat" for "Chitor?" Besides some of the MSS, of the Prithiraj Rásá which are found in Gujrát contain the following prophetic verses. Accordingly the Kutch State in Gujarat can if she please come forward to claim and obtain a decree from the learned researchers of the day, whose experience is sufficiently great and authority undoubted, that this great Epic is fabricated by her sons the Chárans in Sambat year 1942 :—

*Extract.**

कच्छ ही देश सिंधु समध्य, चत्रसेन इक पर्वत सनध्य ।

संवत् अठार आगनीस सोइ, कल्पांत इक संग्राम होइ ।

पासेर भार सव्वा प्रमान, तरहे पषान चहुग्रान रान ।

संवत् अठार छत्तीस जान, कच्छ ही सिन्धु डोलत निधान ।

पर सिंधु बंध कारन प्रमान, इह सुनहि बात चहुग्रान रान ।

कच्छ ही देश भूपाल होइ, शूद्राहि कर्म करिहेति कोइ ।

षट दरस तास न माने अज्ञान, गोहत्या बहोत करिहे निधान ।

संवत् अठार इकताल सोइ, अद्भुत भयंकर काल होइ ।

आगे सुकाल केते सराहे, इकताल समो कीर काल नांहे ।

सततताल बरस कारन सकोइ, कच्छ देश भूप पृथिराज होइ ।

राजान राज करिहे निधान, इह सुनहि बात चहुग्रान रान ।

एकीस बरस इक पुत्र होइ, तपवंत ताहि नवधनति कोइ ।

नवधनह सुत षंगार होइ, संग्राम मध्य मृतकाल होइ ।

---

* See Prithiraj Chohán in Gujarati by Atmárám Keshavji Dvivedi. Second Ed. printed in Sambat 1941 = A. D. 1884 page 126.

बरसहि तास ब्रायस प्रमान, पच्चास इक होइंगे निदान ।

खंगार राज भूपाल होइ, संबत तास ब्रोगनीस सोइ ।

वेहंताल इक ब्रतिक्राल होइ,   *   *   *   *

गठ रयन भूप संग्राम जान, तास पुत्र इक लखपत प्रमान ।

परधान इक चिबंध होइ, जगवीर नाम वाको स कोइ ।

नवघनां सुत खंगार होइ, लखधीर संग ए मंत्र होइ ।

सिधही राज कटिहति कोइ, साम्रथवंत भूपाल होइ ॥

The Substance of the above verses.

In Sambat 1819 a war destructive of the world will take place between Kutch and Sindh countries near the Chatrasen mountain, upon the blood-stream of which a stone $\frac{5}{16}$ of a Seer in weight will float. In Sambat 1836 a second war between the aforesaid countries will ensue. And in Kutch a prince will be born who will do the acts of a Shúdra and will often make cow-slaughter. In Samvat 1841 a great famine will happen—such a one as has not happened before. In Samvat 1847, there will reign a Raja by name Prithiraj. To whom a son namely Nawaghana will be born while he would be 21 years old; who (Nawaghana) in his 51st year will die in battle. In the reign of Khangar Rajá in Sambat 1942 a famine will happen. In his house a son will be born by name Lakhapata. He will be greatly powerful. There will be a minister by name Jagbír. They all three united will conquer the Sindh country &c. &c.

28. The author in proof of the spuriousness of Prithiraj Rásá says that the dates, years, narratives and names of persons in the Epic do not correspond with those given in the Persian histories. But how is it known that all the contents of these Persian histories are quite right? Is there nothing inaccurate in them? Were the writers infallible? If there is any mixture of truth and falsehood in them, how can they go to prove that the great Epic was a gross forgery?

Before making such an extraordinary presumption our author should have first endeavoured his best to make identifications of the names of persons and narratives, and other things mentioned in this great Epic, having gone through all the means available at present in the same way as my venerable tutor Dr. Hoernle has done having had much trouble to achieve a few successes therein. Now let me mention here a few but very useful identifications made by him in his own following words to enable my readers or those who would sit in judgment on the author's attack, and this my humble defence. The learned Doctor says :—

133. "I have but indifferently succeeded in the identification of the warriors of the Sultán. The means at my command were few, such as Major Raverty's Translation of the Tabaqat-i-Nasiri, Sir H. Elliot's History of India, as told by its own (Muhammadan) Historians, &c. Others, who may have a wider acquaintance with Muhammadan authorities, may succeed better. Another drawback is the uncertainty affecting the spelling and identity of so many names in Persian writings, and unfortunately the peculiar antagonism displayed in the notes to Major Raverty's otherwise so valuable work is not calculated to disarm one's distrust. The only two persons whose identity seems beyond question are the Hindú Khán and the Wajiri Khán.

115. Vajír Khán, he was apparently a native of Wajíristán. He is probably identical with Malik, Asad-ud-din, Sher Malik, Wajíri, who is mentioned in the list of the nobles of Shahab-ud-din, in the Tabaqat-i-Nasiri (Major Raverty's Translation) p: 491.

121. Hindú Khán, he was a scion of the Khwárazam Sháhíah dynasty ; the eldest son of Malik Sháh and grandson of Sultán Takish of Khwarazam and Khurásán. He made an attempt to wrest the province of Khurásán from his uncle Sultán Muhammad, but failed ; whereupon he took service with his country's enemy, the Sultáns of Ghor and Gazni. This accounts for his being found on this occasion among the officers of Shahab-ud-din. He is described in the Tabaqat-i-Nasiri (Major Raverty's Translation, pp. 251, 256) as "an exceedingly intrepid, high-minded prince, and endowed with a poetical genius," of which an illustration is given there.

I think also, there cannot be much doubt as to the identity of the Sáhijada (Sáh-zádah "prince," generally "prince royal"). Shahab-ud-din had no son, but only a daughter who died young (Tabaqat, p. 344); but his brother Ghiyaz-ud-din, who was still alive at this time and the paramount Sovereign of the Empire had one son, called Mahmúd, who after the death of his father, was put in charge of the districts of Bust, Isfizár and Faráh by his uncle Shahab-ud-din (See Tabaqat pp. 258, 389, 394, 396, 490, 519, 523) That he should be found, on this occasion accompanying his uncle on his Indian expedition, is not surprising, though it is nowhere noticed in the Tabaqat-i-Nasiri. It is even not impossible that he is mentioned by name in the following line (5 on page 57); Mahamunda may be an error for Mahamuda, (i. e. Mahmúd).

Again the Khilchi Khán is probably the same as the Khalji (or Khalj), Ghiyaz-ud-din, 'Iwaz, who is mentioned as one of Shahab-ud-din's great Generals, and who afterwards became the fourth Sultán of Lakhanawati or Gaur in Bengal (see Tabaqat, pp. 489, 580). There was, however, another Khalji, called Muhamad, son of Mahmúd, in the service of Shahab-ud-din, who is expressly mentioned as having been with him on his later Indian expedition which proved as disastrous to Prithiraj (see Tabacat p. 549). Possibly he may be the Khilchi who is referred to here. According to the Muhammadan historians, in the events of those times, the famous General of Shahab-ud-din, Kutb-ud-din Ibak, is constantly mentioned, in close connection with the Khaljis (see e. g. the list in the Tabaqat, p. 489 also p. 551 ff.) Is it possible, that the Tattár Máruf Khán is identical with him? Kutb-ud-din was a Turk of the Tattár tribe; that name is a mere title, Ibak is a nickname; so that Marúf might have been his personal name. Kutb-ud-din was the Chief of Shahab-ud-din's Generals in his invasions of India, according to the Muhammadan historians; according to Chand, it was Marúf Khán; unless these two persons are indentical, it is strange, that one should be ignored by the Hindú, and the other by the Muhammadan writers.

Again Habas Khán Habasi Hujáb (in S. 40) is probably identical with the person who is called Amir-i-Hájib, Husain-i-

Muhahmmad Hasan in the list of the Tabaqat (p. 491), for some
MSS. read Habashi for Hasan. Perhaps the two Kháns, who are
called Hajarati and Sajarati in V. 38, may be referred to the Malik
Ikhtiyar-un-din, Kharwár and Amir-i-hájib, Husain-i-Surkh in the
list (p. 491), for some of the various readings for Kharwar and
Surkh have some likeness to the Hindi names; and there can be
no doubt that the Persian readings are very corrupt.

195. Hussena Khána Husain Khán) appears to have been a
son of the Mir Husain, who as related in Canto 8, was the primary
cause of the invasions of India by Shahab-ud-din. Mir Husain
or, as he is variously called Sháh Hussain or Husain Khán is there
said to have been a cousin (bandhava) of Shahab-ud-din, a distinguished warrior, living at the Sháh's Court at Gazni. The Sháh
had a beautiful mistress, named Chitrarekhá, to the story of whom
the 10th Canto is devoted. She was fifteen years old and very
skilful in music, and was greatly beloved by the Sháh. Husain
fell in love with her and she with him. One morning the Sháh
sent for him and upbraided him on his conduct. But Husain con-
tinued to intrigue with Chitrarekhá, and was forced to leave the
city. He carried off his family and property and Chitrarekhá, and
fled to Prithiraj to Nagor. Prithiráj, after some hesitation, wel-
comed him and gave him asylum. Hearing of this, Shahab-ud-
din was furious and sent messengers to demand Chitrarekhá from
Husain; failing in which, they were to demand the expulsion of
Husain from Prithiraj. Husain refused to send the woman back,
and Prithiraj replied, he could not give up the man who came to
him for refuge. Shahab-ud-din receiving this answer, at once
prepared to invade India; Prithiraj, on his part also prepared
for war. In the battle that ensued, Husain distinguished
himself greatly, but lost his life. Chamand Rae succeeded in
capturing the Sháh, and thus the battle was decided in favor of
Prithiraj. After five days the Sháh was released and allowed to
return to Ghazni taking Ghazi Husain's son, with him, and pledg-
ing himself no more to make war upon the Hindús. The pledge,
it need hardly be said, was not kept by the Sháh, and the implac-
able hatred, which these events had created in his mind was never

appeased till it was slacked in the blood of Prithiraj and the des-
truction of his Empire. The capture of the Sháh, here related, is
the first of the seven times, he is said to have become the captive of
Prithiraj. The next occasion of his capture is referred to in note
187; once more he is made captive as related in the present Canto.
Chitrarekhá is said to have buried herself with the corpse of Husain.
If the Husain Khán mentioned here, is the son of the elder
Husain, who was taken to Ghazni by Shahab-ud-din, he must
have made his escape afterwards and returned to Prithiraj. The
elder Husain is undoubtedly the same as Nasir-ud-din Husain,
who is repeatedly mentioned in the Tabaqat-i-Nasiri (Major
Ravertys translation, pp. 344, 361, 364 365). He was the older of the
two sons of Malik Shihab-ud-din, Muhammad, a younger brother
of Sultán Bahú-ud-din, Sãm, the father of Sultán Shahab-ud-din.
The elder Husain, therefore, was as Chand correctly states, a cousin
(bandhava) of the latter. In the Tabakat, it is true, it is said
that Nasir-ud-din Husain usurped the throne of his uncle Ala-ud-
din, during the latter's temporary captivity at the Court of Sultán
Sanjar of Khorasan, and that he was murdered by his uncle's par-
tisans on the latter's return from captivity (p. 364). But, firstly,
this story is contradicted by all other Muhammadan historians,
who pass at once from Ala-ud-din to his son (see Major Raverty's
foot-note, p. 364). Secondly, it is more probable that if there was
any usurpation at all, it was made by Nasir-ud-din's father
Muhammad, the younger brother of Ala-ud-din. The three brothers Saif-ud-din Súri, Baha-ud-din Sãm, and Ala-ud-din Husain.
succeeded each other on the throne of Ghor; it is natural, therefore, that during Ala-ud-din's captivity, the fourth brother Shiháb-
ud-din Muhammad, should have occupied or attempted to occupy
the throne. The writer of the Tabaqat must have confused father
and son, as he has done also on other occasions (e. g., with regard
to Ziya-ud-din Muhammad). Thirdly the discription of Nasir-ud-
din Husain's character: "he had a great passion for women and
virgins, and had taken a number of the handmaids and slave girls
of the Sultán's haram" (Tabaqat p. 364), agrees with Chand's story
about his intrigue with Chitrarekhá and has evidently a confused

6

recollection of it. There can, therefore, be little doubt, that Chand gives substantially the true account of Husain's fortunes. It may be added, that both the Tabaqat and other Muhammadan histories give a rather confused relation of an ancestor of this Husain (and of the Ghori royal family generally) who also bore the name of Husain or Hasan, having fled to India, and having lived some time at Delhie (see Tabaqat pp. 322, 323, 332). There is perhaps in this a confused recollection of the flight of Husain to Prithiraj, related by Chand."

29. The author in the conclusion of his paper seconds the statement of Mr. V. A. Smith. "The Rásá, as we have it, is misleading, and all but worthless for the purpose of historians." But it is to be deeply regretted and wondered at—how the author, whose main object in publishing his article in the Society's Journal is to caution the public against the false belief that the Rásá was composed by Chand or any of his contempories, has with assurance omitted to give the foot-note on the passage quoted below of the Editor (A. S. B. J.) and has thereby tried to mislead the readers.

"The great Epic of Chand is hardly sufficiently known as yet to warrant such a sweeping statement." Ed.

Does not the omission of the note in the authors' paper impress the non-subscribers to the Journal of the Society with a false belief and will it not make them think when they have been rightly informed that his opinion and ideas are partial ?

Conclusion.

30. Now I shall give to the world my thoughts, conclusions, and conjectures as to Prithiraj Rásá as we have it at present following in the wake of Antiquarians.

A. The present Prithiraj Rásá has been composed by Chand Bardái the court-bard of Prithiraj the last Hindú and Chohan Emperor of Delhie and Ajmere.

B. I fully agree with the learned researchers such as Messrs. John Beames, B. C. S., F. S. Growse, B. C. S., M. A. and Dr. A. F. R. Hoernle, L.L. D. in thinking that the date of the Rásá was about the twelveth century.

C. The Rásá has no doubt suffered from many additions and alterations by way of interpolation. The statement of my veneable teacher Dr. A. F. R. Hoernle that the grand Epic has passed through three distinct recensions, is to my mind thoroughly correct. I am at one with the Doctor. For, during my residence in the various parts of Rajpootana for about fifteen years, I have made investigation, and come to know of the enimity existing between Chárans on one side, and Raos, Bháts and Barwás on the other for many generations. Sometimes I have had occassion to personally hear their hot animated discussions in the course of which attempts have been made by both the parties to censure and slander each other. I have heard the names of some calumniators among the Charan poets. It is to them that the Ráos impute interpolations in the Rásá. In justice to the Charans I must say that the Ráos too have in return corrupted and disfigured the works of their antagonists. Among the Charans, those poets, who are more learned, opulent and honored than the author, are not of his mind in the matter that the whole of the Rásá going under the name of Chand is a forgery of the 15th or 16th century. But they think with the modern researchers that it has suffered considerably from patch work and interpolation.

31. There is a difference of hundred years between the Sambat era as calculated by Bhats and Geneologists, and used in all their writings and that obtaining in the Shastras. I shall now explain how I have come to know about this Geneologic era. I could not appreciate the merits of the style of the Prithiraj Rásá—nay I undervalued it for some time after I had seen it by Dr. Hoernle at Benares. Ever since I came to Rajputana, I have seen the work read or heard with love and esteem by almost all the Rajas and nobles in all parts of the province. For a time even here I did not like it and looked upon it in the light of my friend the author and poet laureate. Seeing that it commands universal love and veneration in Rajputana, I felt inclined to go through it part by part and examine its merits. While in Kotah I read a portion of it with the famous poet laureate there by name Chandidánji to whom no other Charans of the present time are equal in

Sanskrit. A new light dawned. The Rásá became the centre of attraction and almost all doubts were dispelled from my mind. Then I had a hot discussion as to the dates with the poet laureate, in the presence of Charans and Bháts from Boondee and other places. The result was this—Chandidán affirmed with proof— that at the beginning of the Vickrami era, it was not styled *Sámbat* but *Shak*. But when Shaliwahan having imprisoned and killed Vickramajit, started or founded his own era, the people were in a great stir and excitement. Shaliwahan tried hard that his era might be extant but he saw that it could not supplant, that of Vickrama because the people would not give it up, and as he had granted the request of Vickrama who while in imprisonment having been asked what boon he had to request wished that his era might not be discontinud in public transactions (vide the following quotation from Gladwins Ayeen Akbary :—

"It is said that a youth named Shaliwahan made war upon Bickermajeet and after having taken him prisioner in battle, asked him what boon he had to request? Bickermajeet answered "my only desire is that my era may not be discontinued in public transactions." Shaliwahan granted his request, but at the same time made use of another era from his own accession." Now Shaliwahan ordered that his era should be named "Shak" and that of Vickrama "Sambat" and both remain extant. The Pandits and Astrologers did as they were bid but the Geneologists of Vickrama—the ancesters of the present Charans, Bháts, and Barawas in general—reckoned the "Shak" era of Vickrama from his death as their own in distinction from the above. The difference between these two eras is of 100 years. Between the "Shak" of Shaliwahan and the generally accepted era of Vickrama is 135. The reason of this anomaly is that the Bháts and Geneologists reckoned the age of Vickrama *i. e.,* his life time to be one hundred years. They do not believe that he reigned for 135 years neither do they calculate the time which had most possibly passed before he ascended the throne. Thus two eras of Vickrama became current from this time, one styled the Shástry Sambat accepted by the Pandits and Astrologers and writers of sacred writings, and the other that goes by the name of *Shak* by Bháts and Geneologists. Thus there has been difference of opinion at the fountain head and two parties have sprung up from so early a date. The Bhats used this Bardic Shaka in all their works. The Bardic Shaka (era) remained current pretty well up till the reign of Prithiraj the last Hindú Emperor of Delhie and Ajmere. And the cause of its difference from the Shastry Sambat was known till then. Afterwards its use gradually lessened whereas that of the other increased so much so that all men are now astonished even at hearing it mentioned. The Bardic era is seen more used in the Chohan chronicles than in the histories of other Rajpoot tribes. If we examine the dates as recorded in the Rásá by the standard of the Bardic era, we see them correspond exactly to the other Vickrama era the "Shastry Sambat," only with the uniform difference of one hundred years, and if the same test be applied to the dates both anterior and posterior to the composition of the Rásá we are at once satisfied as to the correctness of our statement. As for instance the Hárá chronicles says that Istapal the founder of the Hárás obtained Aser in S. 981 (1081) and Beesaldeva took possession of Anhulpatan in S. 986 (1086). It is both true and proper that the Bháts should make use of this distinct era—the Bardic Shak—for a man's name is entered in the Geneological Table only at his death—and never before. And all eras so far as they have been yet discovered have been found to originate from a memorable event such as the birth and death of a monarch or a distinguished man, a revolution in religion, installation of a king his dethronement, a great earthquake or a flood. Gladwins' Ayeen Akbary confirms this statement :—

"Every nation forms an era from some memorable event, such as a change in religion ; the accession of one family to the throne upon the extinction or expulsion of another, a great earthquake or a flood."

32. In the great Epic of Chand mistakes have been made by ignorant poets at those times when the work passed through three distinct recensions, in the units and tens of the dates of the Bardic era. I shall now account for them after the learned Courtbard of Kotá.

A. In the verses of Chand यकादश से पंचदह ॥ संवत् इक्क दस पंच श्रग occur. By these the poets who revised the work understood that the year 1115 was meant. The later poets too have done so. This wrong interpretation has made the year 1158, the date of the last battle at Tarain incorrect, for it seems that the poets during the three recensions have found this date by summing up 43 years, the life time of Prithiraj according to the verse चाल्लीस तोंन तिन वर्ष साज to 1115 the year of his birth. But the meaning of Chand seems to be different. By यकादश से पंचदह and संवत् इक्क दस पंच श्रग the poet means 1105. If we add 43 years to this date, we arrive at the right time *i,e.* the Bardic Vickrami Shak 1148, in which the last battle was fought. Now any one may question the truth of this statement and ask the reason why by the word Dasha दश cypher is meant. We say in reply that Dasha दश has both these acceptations. It rests with the poet to use either. In all abstruse, critical and doubtful places which present serious difficulties to a researcher and antiquarian, and are too nice for solution with mathematical precision the common way is to make allowance for any errors even if they be found in dates or in style, and to take pains in sifting all matters with acumen for grasping the possible meaning of the author. If by only adding 43 to 1105 we arrive at the correct date *i. e.* Bardic Sambat 1105+43=1148 then why should we find fault with Chand Bardái by making such a calculation as this that 1115+43=1158.

B. Thus the recensionists have made the year of Prithiraj's going to Kanouj incorrect. When he went to see Kanouj his age, according to the sense conveyed by this verse बरस तोंस छः श्रगारो was 36. The revisers have made an evidently wrong calculation. As 1115+36=1151 which is not the true date. But the author's meaning must have been B. S. 1105+36=1141 the true date.

C. No inaccuracy occurs respecting the date of the first battle of Prithiraj, the year 1140. Only the recensionists have mistaken as to the age of the last Hindú Emperor at the time. They say he was 25 (1115+25=1140) but in reality he was 35 as B. S. 1105+35=1140 shows.

D. During the recensions a great disorder has been made in the date of Prithiraj's adoption and succession to the throne of Delhie. The revisers in their ignorance conjectured that he was 23. They have been so bold as to correct the right date in the original MS. *i. e.* 1115+23=1138. But according to our way of thinking substantiated by the following couplet, his age must have been 8+6=14 years. Because by adding 14 to 1105=1119 the date of Col. Tod S. 1220 is very approximately approached.

दोहा

सित्[1] छ अग्ग सामं सजी । वजि त्रिघोष सुनन्द ।
सोमेसर नन्दन अटल । दिल्ली सुत्रस नरिंद ॥

33. Now according to our hypothesis we shall give against all the verses quoted by the author in his paper such readings or versions of the citations as were genuine or at least expressive of Chand's meaning :—

एकादश से पंच दह ॥

संवत् इक्क दस पंच अग्ग ॥

चालीस तीन तिन वर्षे साज ॥

एकादश संवतह अठ अग्ग हति ईस[2] भनि ॥

ग्यारह से अठ ईस[2] भनि ॥

ग्यारह से अठ ईसा[2] मानं ॥

---

(1) In many of the MSS. now accessible to the public, the word reads Sit सित् but in a MS. of 1770 Sambat, the reading is Sid सिद which seems to me the corruption of Sanskrit Sidhi सिद्धी emblematical of the figure eight. If we take the word to be Sit सित् then the age of Prithiraj becomes either 2 + 6 = 8 or 26. But both of these calculations are highly improper and improbable.

(2) In all MSS. the reading is Tees तीस. But the recensionists have by mistake inserted Tees तीस for Is ईस. By this word Chand in the 30th verse of the Dilli Dán (Gift of Delhi) Canto means eleven—as is seen from the following couplet :—

संवत ईस तीसह अठ । चलि नृप हेम गहि कर कठु ॥

संवत् हर चालीस ॥

ग्यारह से चालीस ॥

ग्यारह इकतालीसवें अथवा ग्यारह से चालीस इक ॥

शाक सुविक्रम सत्त शिव । अध्र[3] उन्न[3] पंचास ॥

एकादश से सत्त अट्ट चालीस अधिकत्तर ॥

34. I maintain, that Ráwal Samarsi was contemporary with, and brother-in-law to Prithiraj Chohán, Emperor of Delhie and Ajmere. The inscriptions quoted by the author, do not satisfy me, with the correctness of dates, mentioned therein. They confirm my statement, conjectural of course,—that some self-interested persons had them engraved, years after the death of Samarsi,—either the dates were written from a failing memory, or those of another Samarsi,—Rao Rájá of Boondi, were inserted by mistake, consequent on the confusion of names. The time of the inscriptions, alluded to by the author, was the time of this Samarsi, who flourished some 45 or 46 years after his more illustrious name sake of Mewar. I shall give a brief account of this Boondi Rájá, for the edification of my readers. The coincidence of names is not a thing to be wondered at, for it must have originated, from the esteem in which Samarsi a great hero, both in camp and council was held. To H. H. the Ráo Rájá Shri Rámsingh Ji Bahádur G. C. S. I. of Boondi—a prince deeply versed in Sanskrit, experienced in all the intricacies of government for the long, now unusual period of 65 years, and himself a depositary of the annals and antiquities of Raputáná, my thanks are due for his kindly

---

Here in this quotation they have made another mistake by writing Tísaru तीसरु in place of Isaru ईसरु. The correct reading is as follows :—

संवत् ईस ईसरु अट्ठ । बलि नृप हेम गहि कर कट्टु ॥

(3) During the recensions, the word Adhra अध्र a corruption of the Sanskrit Adhara अधर emblematical of two suffered much from the wrong orthography in vogue in Rajputana. In the several stages of its corruption the word passed from अद्ध the latest form of अध्र to अट्ठ and is sufficiently misleading to one not acquainted with the defective practice. Besides the word Unna उन्न is by mistake written Agga अग्ग for the people here are in the habit of pronouncing and writing अ for उ or ई.

giving me the use of the histories (1) of his family and many
other valuable information—I learn from the Geneological Table
of the Hárá Kings that Samarsi was born to Devaráj, in S. 1293.
His father out of great love and affection to him divided the
whole Kingdom into two parts, the first he named the principality
of Bambávadá, and kept it to himself, while the second that of
Boondi, he gave to him, and made him King in S. 1300, when he
was but seven. In S. 1310, his heir apparent Nápáji was born
and he extended the town of Boondi in Sambat year of 1320. In
the next year, the city of Kotá was founded. In S. 1328 * he
availed himself of the attack of the Delhie Emperor on Chitore,
and wrested Mandalgarh from Mewar. In S. 1332 * in a battle
with the Emperor, he was killed with his father Devaráj.

Now it must be admitted, that the discovery of a second
Samarsi, makes the position of our author, very unstable and
insecure, inasmuch as his age tallies with the time of the inscriptions, and his hand was seen in Mewar, for he had often come
in contract with this great ancient Kingdom. Besides in the
Geneological Tables of the Mewar Kings, which go by the name of
Khyáta, (ख्यात), and which are in the possession of every respectable family in Mewar, it is written, that the date of Ráwal
Samarsi's accession to the throne, and that of his death are respectively S. 1106 and 1148. Now the Kaviráj's statement that the
Prithiraj Rásá alone, has occasioned mistakes, in all the Histories
and Geneological Tables in India, be supposed to be true, we at
once see the absurdity of this supposition, for how could the Epic
of the day be made responsible for the mistakes, when its date of
the death of Samarsi is S. 1158. To arrive at the true time, we
must either take the 1 in the hundred's place, to be a numerical
error, for the figure 1 and 2 in Sanskrit and Hindi can easily be
confused, or account for it in the way I have done, i. e. by the
presumption of the Bárdie era.

(1) Vansha Prakásha and Vansha Bháskar.
* Some Mss. of Khyáts ख्यात have S. 1338 for 1328, and S. 1342
for 1332.

7

35. I cannot conclude this work more fitly than by quoting the following passages of Col. Tod in appreciation of Prithiraj Rásá :—

"The work of Chand is a universal history of the period in which he wrote. In the sixty-nine books, comprising one hundred thousand stanzas, relating to the exploits of Prithiraj, every noble family of Rajasthan will find some record of their ancestors. It is accordingly treasured amongst the archives of each race having any pretension to the name of Rajpoot. From this he can trace his martial forefathers who 'drank the wave of battle' in the passes of Kirman, when 'the cloud of war rolled on Himachil' to the plains of Hindusthan. He was of Prithiraj, his alliances, his numerous and powerful tributaries, their abodes and pedigrees make the works of Chand invaluable as historic and geographical memoranda, besides being treasures in mythology, manners and the annuals of the mind. To read this poet well is a sure road to honor, and my own Goorú was allowed, even by the professional bards to excel therein. As he read I rapidly translated about thirty thousand stanzas. Familiar with the dialects in which it is written, I have fancied that I seized occasionally the poets spirit; but it were presumtion to suppose that I embodied all his brilliancy or fully comprehended the depth of his allusions. But I know for whom he wrote. The most familiar of his images and sentiments I heard daily from the mouths of those around me, the descendants of the men whose deeds he rehearses. I was enabled thus to seize his meaning where one more skilled in poetic lore might have failed, and to make my prosaic version of some value."